PRAISE FOR

"I contacted [Robin after] a wonderful friend of mine bought 3 healings for me to see if it would help. I was constantly stressed out and always on edge. I just didn't know what to do anymore. I have been on meds, went to counseling, therapy, you name it I have done it. I have 3 small children and run an organization as well. Life was just becoming overwhelming and I was always miserable. I also have Narcolepsy, depression, and a small case of OCD. I was hesitant to contact Robin thinking could this really work? I mean how in the world could she help me from the comfort of her home when she is hundreds of miles away? But I figured at this point I would do almost anything just to have some peace. I am SO glad I did. My stress level has greatly decreased. My relationship with my fiancé has changed for the better because of that as well. I have NO clue how it works but I can tell you IT DOES. I want to thank Robin for everything she is truly amazing! " — JS

"I have an Autistic daughter and she received a healing from Robin Linke and I cannot sing enough Praise. Finally someone who is passionate in healing for special needs children and others". — TG

"Who would've thought the shift from Malcolm X to Gandhi! LOL. Seriously, I feel my insides shifting and I have lost some seriously stubborn belly fat. I guess it's the energy moving thru the sacral and solar plexus chakras? All I know is ever since the Reiki Diva Robin started working on me, I have a much more peaceful disposition. I used to be the "Fire and Brimstone" type. Now, I'm speaking "Love and Peace". *shock* Am I perfect? Hell to the No. But I am cool with that and with who I am becoming. Like Michael said: "It's all good" :D" — EB

"You give so much value in your readings and your guidance I appreciate all the time and energy you spend to help me. You tell it how it is and give me courage to take the steps I need to take to accomplish what I want to achieve! Thank you for helping me along my journey. You are amazing! " — WD

"The insight you've given me, as well as the shifting that's taken place because of the Theta work, has been gently profound (ie: simple, yet powerful). Luv UUUUUUUUUU! " — MC

"I love you Robin! Your insight and clearing abilities have helped me so much in my life. God sent me a gift yesterday I've been asking for for three years! The Happiest day!! xo — AB

"I am 15 years old and very scared of public high school after being home schooled. My mom bought me a session with Robin and like WOW totally different. I now have confidence I can do this. She still talks to me weekly and I am so blessed to have her Thanks Robin :) " — JB

"My 2 year old granddaughter is like a new person with me tonight… happy, a kid again… running around… .light hearted… my gosh… .how can I ever thank you… " — GP

"I came into this world with a variety of health challenges and I have had Reiki healing before, but Robin has surpassed all of previous encounters. Her acute sensitivity to my body's energy, along with her highly intelligent communication skills, makes working with her an experience that has mentally and physically enhanced my life. " — VM

"I'd never experienced any type of pain relief for my knee other than popping pills and getting shots. Since that first session, you have performed Reiki, IET and other Theta sessions on me, and every time I feel better, not only physically, but emotionally as well. You have done more to help free my mind from emotional crap than all my years of therapy combined. A "healing" from the other side of the continent??? I was abundantly skeptical. The energy surge I felt from 3000 miles away as you did "Theta" on me removed any doubt that energy work was real. I thank you from the bottom of my open and healing heart. " — DR

PRAISE FOR ROBIN'S HEALING JEWELRY

"Robin, I just wanted to let you know that my gorgeous bracelet arrived a couple of days ago and it is amazing! The beautiful energy I felt when I put it on was so strong and loving. This is my second piece from you and I just wanted to say thank you so much for the love and care you put into them. Much love and hugs xoxoxo" — SM

"My new bracelet. It's beautiful!!!! I have to tell you that I had a dream about my asthma being healed last week by a blue bracelet. I told my mom about my dream, it must have been right after she ordered it from you, she just laughed. I thought it was because she thought my dream was funny. Anyway, now I know why she was laughing about my dream. Thank you so much again for sharing your gift! " — TB

"Your work is not only beautiful, you put so much of you into it you can feel it the second you hold it in your hand. I am so very grateful to have found you. :) — LS

"I received my bracelet today!! I love it! I felt the energy from it as soon as I opened the box! Thank you Robin for sharing your gift with those of us that need healing! " — JG

"YOU ROCK! ROBIN, I love the energy, intention and pure spiritual essence of your jewelry work! It's simply stunning and spiritually inspired! " — RB

"I received my energized jewelry last night… as soon as I opened the package… . the smell of the sage was wonderful. Thank you so much… I wanted to sleep in it! I'm wearing it again today… with my sweats and socks on, and loving them… they truly are more beautiful in person. Thank you again, and thank you for the energy… it is very uplifting. " — JL

"I absolutely love my bracelet and I have worn it every day since it arrived. " — MW

"I received my beautiful jewelry from you last week, and I wanted to thank you for it. I am very happy with both gorgeous pieces. Please keep making more amazing jewelry. " — BP

"Thank you. I want to tell you that my daughter has really felt a lot better since stealing and wearing my bracelet and she refuses to take it off. She's convinced it is her miracle bracelet. " — CK

"I love your jewelry. the prosperity necklace is amazing! so far I've gotten a raise at work and some of the back unemployment that I fought for from last year. " — LZ

"Oh yes yes yes its perfect! Thank you a million times over. It's so beautiful. Bless you Robin." — ES

Also by Robin Linke

Angel and Gemstone Guidance Cards
25 laminated wallet sized cards with messages from the angels. Includes corresponding crystals.

Custom Healing Jewelry

Healing Sessions
ThetaHealing®
Angelic IET®
Reiki
The Kitchen Sink

Intuitive Readings

Workshops and Classes
Energy Work for Autism
Healing and Jewelry Parties

The Little Book of BIG Insights

Volume I

Tips and Tricks for living a life of Joy, Abundance, and Ease

Robin Linke

U¹⁰
You 10 Publishing

The Little Book of BIG Insights
Volume I
Tips and Tricks for living a life of Joy, Abundance, and Ease
Robin Linke

ISBN: 978-0-9848642-1-8

Copyright © 2011 Robin Linke. All Rights Reserved.

www.RobinLinke.com

Cover, design and Wolf Logo by
Dichotomy Design
www.DichotomyDesign.com

Cover Photograph: Mariel Pietrykoski

No part of this book may be reproduced, stored in or introduced into a retrieval system, or transmitted, in any form or by any means (electronic, mechanical, photocopying, recording or otherwise), without the prior written permission of the publisher and copyright owner. Without limiting those rights, the author and publisher grant limited sharing specifically of the 150 Tips and Tricks ("tips") in your *public online posts* strictly under the provisions that you:
   a) Share no more than one (1) tip per post.
   b) Provide clear attribution to Robin Linke on each and every post.
   c) Only use for noncommercial purposes. If you charge people to view your Web site or blog or want to use any of this content in any for-profit publication, you'll have to ask for explicit permission.
   d) Do not modify (make "derivatives"). Use only the entire "tip".

The author of this book does not dispense medical advice or prescribe the use of any technique as a form of treatment for physical, emotional, or medical problems without the advice of a physician, either directly or indirectly. The intent of the author is only to offer information of a general nature to help you in your question of emotional and spiritual well-being. In the event you use any of the information in this book for yourself, which is your constitutional right, the author and the publisher assume no responsibility for your actions.

U^{10}
You 10 Publishing

This book is dedicated to my two dearest friends and most devoted supporters, David Rosenhaus and Prakash Menon. Their wisdom, love, magic and unwavering belief in me is one of the greatest and most treasured gifts I have ever received. From the depths of my heart and soul I thank you both for finding me and being such an important part of my life.

Introduction

Hello and welcome! I'm so excited to see you here! Really, I am. You're probably wondering why. I mean we may not even know each other (at least not consciously). My dream is to see people discover that life is full of possibilities and miracles. When you realize that, you can co-create a life of joy, abundance, and ease. This is not to say that "bad" things will never happen, but you will be better equipped to handle and move through them. So yes, I really am excited to see you here.

In this book, I share things that I have found to be true for me and my clients. Having said that, I would also like to acknowledge that we are each on our own unique journey and what may be true for some may not be true for others. I ask that you view these insights, tips, and tricks with an open mind and open heart. Try them on for size and see how they feel to you.

How To Use This Book:

There is no right or wrong way to use this book. You can choose from the suggestions below and see what resonates, or discover your own personal methods. Heck you can use the book as a coaster if that's what works for you. This is your journey and these are your choices.

I. With the book closed, ask in your heart or out loud what you need to know for the day. Open the book and read the first message your eye lands on.
II. If you have a specific question that you're looking for clarity on, keep the book closed, ask a question and open the book to see what insights it has to offer. Keep in mind that the insight may not be your answer, instead it may point you in the direction of the answer.
III. Read the book straight through.
IV. Choose to read one insight daily.
V. Pick one insight and meditate on it.

References Throughout the Book

I refer to several tools throughout the book. If you aren't familiar with them, here is a quick reference guide for you. This is my way of working with them. You might find different ways to make them yours.

CRYSTALS:

I love working with crystals and stones. They each carry a unique vibration that can aide you on your journey. When working with crystals, use them as you feel guided. I have mine with me all the time. They sit on the night stand by my bed. I have some in my workspace, healing space, and living space. I keep them in my pocket and in my handbag. I've even gone so far as to create a line of gemstone healing jewelry so that I can carry my crystals with me and look stylish too. You can also meditate with the crystals or even ask them questions (I do). The more time you spend with your crystals, the better your results.

Crystals (like people) take on the energies from their environments. It's for this reason that they should be energetically cleansed on a regular basis. You'll know when it's time to cleanse them. For example, they may not feel very good to you or you may notice that the energy is not as strong. You may also notice a change in their appearance or just get an intuitive nudge telling you they need some attention. I find the easiest and most effective way of clearing crystals is by smudging them. Smudging is a method that's been around for hundreds and thousands of years. If you're not familiar with smudging, I describe it in the Smudging and Cleansing section of this book *(see page vi)*.

Angels:

When I talk about angels, I'm referring to energies that are an aspect of Source, Creator, God, the Divine, the Universe (or insert the name of your Divinity here). They do not carry a religious connation for me. My way of working with the angels is very loose and open. I simply converse with them as I would anyone or anything else.

Grounding:

Grounding is a tool I use often, if not daily, to help co-create the life I desire. It helps you to be present and connected in the moment and with the earth plane.

You can ground by sitting outside on the grass (or any other natural surface... boulders are awesome) and allowing yourself to fully take notice of how the ground feels beneath you. How it supports you. Be aware of the sights and sounds around you and find the beauty and peace of the moment. If you're able, lean against a tree while doing this and it will add to your experience.

You can also try the following grounding meditation.

GROUNDING MEDITATION

Sit comfortably with your feet flat on the floor. Close your eyes and breathe deep into your lower belly. Allow your body to begin to relax. Notice any areas of your body that are tense. Breathe into those areas knowing that you are breathing in the energy of peace and calm. As you continue breathing, allow your body to start feeling heavy. With the heaviness comes more peace. You are relaxing into your body and being. Imagine your feet are rooted to the earth. See tree roots growing out from the bottom of your feet into the rich nurturing soil of mother earth. Watch as the roots grow deeper and deeper... attaching you more firmly to our loving mother earth. Feel the soil envelop those roots and feed them with healing energies. Feel how welcoming this energy truly is. Sit quietly for a few moments allowing yourself to be fully nurtured and loved. Allow your body to continue to get heavier and heavier and relax more and more. Keep breathing. Remain here for another 30 seconds to 5 minutes. Whatever feels most comfortable for you. If any thoughts cross your mind thank them for showing up and ask them to leave. You can visit with them later.

Now, begin pulling up the loving, healing, peaceful earth energy and allow it to fill your entire being. Keep pulling it up… more… more… that's it.

Bring your awareness back to your breath now. Start becoming aware of your body. Notice the sounds around you. Wiggle your fingers and your toes… and as you're ready, open your eyes knowing that even though your feet are rooted to the earth, you can reach the heavens and beyond, just as a tree does. You can reach all areas of the Universe, just as the seedlings from the trees do… and you can grow anywhere you desire. All it takes is love and nurturing.

A free MP3 of this guided meditation can be played or downloaded at www.RobinLinke.com/groundingmeditation

Smudging and Cleansing

As you go about your day, you come in contact with innumerable energies. Most, if not all, are energies that are not beneficial to you. They can create confusion within you, or make you think you're angry, sad, etc. Most of the time, you don't even know that these energies don't belong to you, and if you do, you may have a hard time shaking them off. It's for this reason that I highly suggest energetically cleansing yourself daily. If you are unable to find the time to do it daily, forget to do it daily, or just plain don't want to do it daily, no worries. Just as with everything else in this book, these are the Truths that I have found to be most effective for me and my clients. It doesn't mean that you HAVE to do things MY way. Do what works for you. Keeping that in mind, below are the two ways that I find to be easiest and most effective when it comes to cleansing.

SMUDGING

Of all the different kinds of sage (there are over 750 species worldwide), I prefer white sage for smudging. It's best to smudge with intent, so before lighting your sage, say a few words or a prayer asking for unwanted or unneeded energy to be released.

You can smudge your living space, your belongings, your car, your energy field, your crystals or even your pets.

White sage emits a lot of smoke, so it's recommended that you open a window in the area you are smudging in, especially if you have lung issues. If that's the case, you can keep some sage with you in a small pouch as a form of protection against unwanted energies, or you can have someone else smudge your home while you are out. Another option is to purchase smudging spray and use that instead.

Place a few leaves of white sage in an abalone shell, or any heat resistant container and light it. Let it flame for a few seconds and gently blow it out. You'll be left with white, purifying smoke. Walk around your space and fan the smoke knowing that all unneeded energies are being released.

Once you're done, you can say a few words or prayer of gratitude if you like. That's it. Your space and you will feel a whole lot better.

SALT BATH

Salt baths are a wonderful, relaxing, nurturing, simple way of cleansing your energy field. Drop a handful of sea salt into your tub as it's filling with warm water. Choose the type of sea salt that works for you. There's the sea salt you can purchase at the grocery store, there's Himalayan sea salt, dead sea salt and more. You can choose a coarse or fine grain. This is all a matter of personal taste. The bottom line is that it's the sea salt that cleanses your energy field.

You can also include a handful of Epsom salts if you desire. This will act as an aide in the detoxification process. You can add a few drops of lavender essential oil for relaxation or some sweet orange essential oil for an uplifting energy. Or rose oil to bring in the energy of love. Have fun with it! Create! Experiment!

You may want to consider lighting some candles and putting on relaxing music to add to the atmosphere. Soak in the tub for at least 10 minutes. Personally, I find the longer I soak the better, simply because I find it highly relaxing.

If you don't like baths, combine fine sea salt with honey to make a paste. Add a drop or two of essential oil if you want, and use it as a body scrub.

May this book bring you joy as you follow the road to magic and miracles.

Abundant Blessings,

Robin

1

Rather than Aspiring to be like someone else, what if you Conspire to be yourself? Conspire with the Universe to create situations that allow you to be yourself.

Tips and Tricks for living a life of Joy, Abundance, and Ease

2

Look at your belief systems, behaviors and actions. Pick one that is not serving you and work at letting it go. Remember to have compassion for yourself during the process.

Tips and Tricks for living a life of Joy, Abundance, and Ease

3

Endings are a way of creating space for something that you desire such as a new job, a new relationship, or even a new way of life. Bless the endings, bless the lessons, bless whatever new is coming in.

4

Staying out of guilt and resentment helps you move through transformation with less pain, suffering and drama.

Tips and Tricks for living a life of Joy, Abundance, and Ease

5

Take the time to see your gifts. Do you recognize them? Your gifts enrich people's lives. I'm challenging you today to look for and discover your gifts.

Tips and Tricks for living a life of Joy, Abundance, and Ease

6

You are the co-creator of your life. While things may happen around you, how they affect you is up to you. What do you choose?

Tips and Tricks for living a life of Joy, Abundance, and Ease

7

Do you forget about self love when you're feeling down? Isn't that when you want to take better care of your heart and soul? What can you do to remind your heart and soul that You love You?

Tips and Tricks for living a life of Joy, Abundance, and Ease

8

Find small pockets of time to do something that feeds your soul. The more often you do this, the more you will begin to feel fulfilled.

Tips and Tricks for living a life of Joy, Abundance, and Ease

9

The Universe is abundant. Rather than focus on what you CAN'T buy or what you're unable to do, keep your eye on the big picture. As long as you have breath in your body, you can work at co-creating the reality that is perfect for you. Simple? Yes. Easy? Not always. Pay attention to signs and road blocks in order to determine your next move... which may simply be to just be.

10

Live your life with passion, compassion, and gratitude. Anything less is just survival.

Tips and Tricks for living a life of Joy, Abundance, and Ease

11

Scent is an easy way to adjust the energy in your home or work space. Try diffusing essential oils. Cinnamon, pine, vanilla or pumpkin spice are great scents for creating a homey atmosphere. Orange, grapefruit, and rosemary are clean, uplifting scents which help clear your mind and lighten the energy.

12

It's difficult to rise above life's challenges until you recognize and accept that on some level there is a lesson in them. Once you do that, you will begin to release yourself from the space of victim-hood and begin living life from the heart.

Tips and Tricks for living a life of Joy, Abundance, and Ease

13

The difference between living and surviving is nothing more than changing your point of view. You have the power to choose love over fear and no one can make the choice for you.

Tips and Tricks for living a life of Joy, Abundance, and Ease

14

Your true purpose is to live a joyful life in spite of the drama. Embrace your challenges, thank the Universe for the lessons received (even if you don't know what they are) and LIVE joyfully.

Tips and Tricks for living a life of Joy, Abundance, and Ease

15

People just want to be seen. Take an extra second today to make eye contact with the clerk at the grocery store. Smile and really say hello. Hold the door open for someone, make eye contact and smile. Walk with your head up. SEE people around you. Sometimes that's all that's needed to change the vibration of their day and yours.

16

Unplug from the drama and breathe through your challenges. Feel your emotions but wait until the worst has passed before acting or reacting. No matter what happens outside of you, you ALWAYS have a choice when it comes to your actions and reactions.

Tips and Tricks for living a life of Joy, Abundance, and Ease

17

Give yourself a vacation from your stuff. When you get too buried in your stuff – fears, worries, obsessive thoughts – you lose sight of the big picture.

18

No one is so busy that they can't take 15 or even 5 minutes to practice self love. Look in the mirror and say "I love you". If that is too difficult (and it is for many) try arriving at your appointments 5 minutes early and use the time to sit, be fully present, and breathe.

Tips and Tricks for living a life of Joy, Abundance, and Ease

19

Your voice is one of the strongest tools you have at your disposal. Use it to change your vibration. Use it wisely and with emotion. Yelling and arguing rocket lower vibrating energies out to the Universe. Chanting and singing rocket higher vibrating energies out to the Universe. By the way, singing works even if you think your singing stinks.

20

Are you trying to manifest? Turn your manifestation or prayer into a song and sing it out loud.

Tips and Tricks for living a life of Joy, Abundance, and Ease

21

What does your soul want you to focus on today? Does it want you to rest? Then rest. Not honoring the soul's needs causes you to be out of alignment with your true self which then creates more challenges in your life.

Tips and Tricks for living a life of Joy, Abundance, and Ease

22

eeling down? Make a list of all the things you love to do and see how your vibration changes. It's simply amazing how the act of writing these activities down improves your mood. Remember, you are simply focusing on what you love to do, not on thoughts such as not having the time, money, etc. to do them.

Tips and Tricks for living a life of Joy, Abundance, and Ease

23

Let your inner child out to play. Bake and decorate cupcakes--just because. Paint, skip, play hopscotch. The key is to take a break and have some fun. Jump out of your comfort zone and play, play, play... even if it's only in your imagination. Kids love daydreaming, take a moment to indulge your inner child.

Tips and Tricks for living a life of Joy, Abundance, and Ease

24

Smile for no reason today... as much and as often as possible. (The side benefit to this is that people will begin to wonder what you're up to).

Tips and Tricks for living a life of Joy, Abundance, and Ease

25

Put on some fun, loud music and sing. Your vibration will entrain to that of the music and will start to rise. Singing gives your mind something to concentrate on other than your problems.

26

Spend time listening to your soul today. What is it saying? What is it asking for? Find a quiet place clear of distractions. Close your eyes and take a few deep breaths. Place your hand over your heart and ask it a question. Be sure to give it permission to answer. Or, you can simply invite your heart to speak to you.

27

Get your body moving. Do you like to exercise? Exercise raises your endorphin levels which has been proven to improve your mood. If you don't like to exercise, then dance. You can dance and pretend it's not really exercise.

Tips and Tricks for living a life of Joy, Abundance, and Ease

28

If you're having trouble sleeping, here is a great combination of stones to place under your pillow at night: amethyst, sodalite, and howlite Amethyst is a purple stone that carries meditative energies. Sodalite is a blue stone which quiets and calms the mind. Howlite is a white stone and is THE best stone to use if you're having trouble sleeping.

For more info on using crystals, see page iii.

Tips and Tricks for living a life of Joy, Abundance, and Ease

29

When making decisions don't forget your intuition. Intuition is one of your most reliable sources of information. Tap into it often.

Tips and Tricks for living a life of Joy, Abundance, and Ease

30

When receiving information from anyone, including spiritual teachers, use your discernment to determine if what they say is true for you. There is no one "right" way to follow your path.

Tips and Tricks for living a life of Joy, Abundance, and Ease

31

Do the "why"s really matter? You are where you are. If you are happy, you are happy. If you are in need of healing, you are in need of healing. The "why"s do not change that.

32

Take time to reassess your relationships. Not just your relationships with other people, but also your relationship with yourself, your job, money, security and so on. What's working for you and what isn't? If a relationship isn't working, decide whether you'd like to work on it, or let go of it. Letting go can be hard, but it makes room for something new to show up.

33

People often react to situations and experiences out of habit. The next time you catch yourself reacting to a situation, check in and see if it's how you really feel or if you too are reacting from habit.

34

Give yourself permission to succeed. Giving yourself permission may include succeeding in a way you never imagined. It may include looking at your beliefs. Do you hold the belief that if you succeed you won't have time for your family anymore? Are you concerned that success may change your relationship with your significant other? Do you feel that you're actually worthy or deserving of success?

Tips and Tricks for living a life of Joy, Abundance, and Ease

35

Sometimes your soul uses outside sources to speak. Maybe you'll catch a few words from someone else's conversation. You might find your answer in the song playing on the radio. These are just a few of the ways your soul finds its voice.

36

If you'd like to create a new beginning, dream it. Then tap into the Wisdom of the Universe via your Spirit Connection and ask for the dream. Then take the actions you're shown so you can actualize it.

Tips and Tricks for living a life of Joy, Abundance, and Ease

37

Doing something you love is food for the soul. A soul that's been properly fed has more to give and share with others. What do you love to do? Make some time to do it without fear, regret, or worry.

38

Do you pick up on other people's feelings? Do you often feel other people's pain? This can become overwhelming and exhausting. Remember to ground your energies often, especially when you're going to be around large groups of people.

For the grounding exercise, see page iv.

Tips and Tricks for living a life of Joy, Abundance, and Ease

39

When you're feeling overwhelmed in any way, the emotions and feelings you're experiencing may not be your own. Ask yourself: "Is this mine?" Wait a moment and then say: "I return this to sender with love". Returning the energy to sender with love gives it the opportunity to transmute. You may have to do this a few times until you get used to it, but you'll begin to feel much lighter.

40

When the energy of transformation is around, it creates situations that feel almost like they're forcing you to let go of what's not working or what isn't needed. Take a look at your current challenges and work at finding a new way of doing things.

Tips and Tricks for living a life of Joy, Abundance, and Ease

41

Fixing our friends and loved ones is not the same as supporting them. Fixing sends the message that we don't accept them as they are. Supporting them is being loving and compassionate no matter who they are. Sometimes people need to make their own mistakes in order to grow. One way we can support people is through guidance. However, we cannot force others to accept or receive our guidance.

42

Look for the true prosperity in your life. While money is necessary for the world we live in, prosperity comes in many forms. People, animals, indoor plumbing... the more you are able to see and appreciate the gifts you already have, the easier it will be for you to accept more and varied gifts into your life.

Tips and Tricks for living a life of Joy, Abundance, and Ease

43

Let go of the pain from your past. Send wishes for the future to the angels and allow them to manifest in the way that is right for you... appreciate the present moment and live your life in the now.

44

Practice discernment when receiving messages from your guides and angels. Having faith in their guidance does not mean you have to follow it blindly. Free will is your birthright.

Tips and Tricks for living a life of Joy, Abundance, and Ease

45

Answers and guidance come to us when we least expect them. Be patient and know you will receive your messages when you are ready on all levels... and sometimes in the most unexpected of ways.

Tips and Tricks for living a life of Joy, Abundance, and Ease

46

Live your life in a way that aligns with your True Self. Some moments you are able to make better choices than others. You make the best choices you're capable of in each moment.

Tips and Tricks for living a life of Joy, Abundance, and Ease

47

Life is full of dichotomies. We're told "don't sweat the small stuff", followed by "it's all in the details". We're reminded to "live in the moment", yet we need to set our alarm clocks in order to wake up in time for work. It's finding the balance in these dichotomies that allows your spirit and body to live together harmoniously.

Tips and Tricks for living a life of Joy, Abundance, and Ease

48

Accepting your physical body and its physical state is essential to being a well balanced person. Ask your body what it requires from you to be healthy. Bless it, thank it for housing your soul and honor it in a way that is right for you and it.

Tips and Tricks for living a life of Joy, Abundance, and Ease

49

Follow YOUR dreams and not the dreams you believe you're supposed to follow. Following another's dream may seem like you're being selfless, but you're not. You're diminishing yourself, instead.

50

The highest way to deal with those who attack us is to respond with love and compassion. We have no clue what their past programming is, or what kind of day they've had. Responding to anger with anger breeds more anger. That's not to say you should be a doormat, but you can state your peace and stand your ground from a place of love instead.

Tips and Tricks for living a life of Joy, Abundance, and Ease

51

Let go of your attachment to the outcome and allow for what's in your highest and best good to come in. Stop thinking about what you "think" will happen and allow for the possibilities.

Tips and Tricks for living a life of Joy, Abundance, and Ease

52

Did you remember to practice your spiritual hygiene today? Make clearing and grounding a part of your daily routine like brushing your teeth.

For grounding techniques, see page iv.
For cleansing techniques, see page vi.

Tips and Tricks for living a life of Joy, Abundance, and Ease

53

Life's surprises are simply ways to either bring illumination to a challenge... or to light the way to your next best step. If fear is getting in your way, try connecting with a piece of charoite. Charoite is a wonderful crystal that aids in releasing fear.

For more info on using crystals, see page iii.

Tips and Tricks for living a life of Joy, Abundance, and Ease

54

Have you set an intention for the day? Setting an intention is just another way to put the law of attraction into play. Set it and forget it… at the end of the day, observe what happened.

Tips and Tricks for living a life of Joy, Abundance, and Ease

55

Find time to be quiet and disengage. Instead of "decompressing" in front of the tv, take 30 minutes to sit in a warm sea salt bath. Don't forget to light some candles and play music you love too.

Tips and Tricks for living a life of Joy, Abundance, and Ease

56

Each day, each moment, each second is one we've never ever experienced before. Although they may appear similar to other moments we've experienced, they are not. How cool is that?

Tips and Tricks for living a life of Joy, Abundance, and Ease

57

Learning to accept experience as the sacred gift it is will help you to transform with more ease and less fear.

Tips and Tricks for living a life of Joy, Abundance, and Ease

58

Be who you really are. Honor the beautiful person that you are. "Changing" in order to fit someone else's idea of who they believe you should be does not serve you or the other person.

Tips and Tricks for living a life of Joy, Abundance, and Ease

59

Performing small acts of selfless kindness creates magic in your life and in the life of those you assist.

60

etting go of obsessions allows your intuition to shine through and light the way to your next best steps. Moonstone is a lovely crystal to have around for increasing your intuitive awarenesses.

For more info on using crystals, see page iii.

Tips and Tricks for living a life of Joy, Abundance, and Ease

61

Spend some time being present with your thoughts today. Notice if you tend to think one thing and back it up with an action or another thought that says just the opposite.

62

When asking the Universe for anything you must be clear in your intention... in both word and thought. Send out your wish and detach from the outcome. Don't forget to let the Universe know that you are open to receiving your wish or something even better.

63

Are you addicted to negative thought patterns? Do you only see what "can't" be done? Do you only notice what you "don't" have? Do you focus only on who is not supportive of you? Find your gratitude to cancel those thought patterns. What are you grateful for? Find one thing, focus on it. Let it fill your heart and soul...... now breathe...... isn't that better?

64

In trying to control every aspect of another's life, you deny them the opportunity to learn how to find their own answers. They may also miss experiences that could have led them in a new direction or resulted in a valuable lesson.

Tips and Tricks for living a life of Joy, Abundance, and Ease

65

Forgiving someone who has hurt or "wronged" you is not the same as letting yourself be treated like a doormat. Forgiving is simply letting go of the emotional charge attached to the person or situation.

66

Surrendering does not mean that you don't have choices or options. Surrender is not weakness. Surrender is based in love and faith. Weakness is based in fear.

Tips and Tricks for living a life of Joy, Abundance, and Ease

67

If you want to experience abundance, act abundant. Pretend you're abundant. If you don't know what abundance looks or feels like, ask the Universe to show you.

Tips and Tricks for living a life of Joy, Abundance, and Ease

68

Call on Archangel Raphael to aid you in your healing. He helps heal all aspects of your life, including relationships and situations. No special prayers needed. Just think of him and ask for help.

For info on angels, see page iv.

69

Angels love to help us, and are able to be in all places at all times. No task is too big or too small. However, they cannot do anything without our request. Call on your angels, ask for help, be ready and willing to receive.

For info on angels, see page iv.

Tips and Tricks for living a life of Joy, Abundance, and Ease

70

If you don't have the monetary resources to help someone in need, look for other ways to be of service. Volunteer, donate unused items, or share your favorite charity with your friends. They may have the resources to help, or know someone who does.

71

Be generous with your Light. Shine it everywhere. The interesting thing about this practice is that some people won't like it if you walk around happy, smiling, and spreading love. Rather than judge yourself as wrong, recognize that they are unable or not ready to receive that sort of energy. The more you allow yourself to shine, the more of that energy is put out to the Universe which creates a situation where more people will be willing to receive it.

72

You may not like the choices that are available to you. That's okay. Just pick something.

Tips and Tricks for living a life of Joy, Abundance, and Ease

73

What if mistakes were actually experiences that allowed you to learn something new? Maybe they taught you an ineffective way of doing something. Maybe they showed you a different way of reaching your destination. Maybe they opened the door to a wonderful possibility that hasn't appeared yet.

Tips and Tricks for living a life of Joy, Abundance, and Ease

74

If you don't treat yourself with love and compassion, chances are, others won't either. Instead, choose to treat yourself as you would a treasured friend.

Tips and Tricks for living a life of Joy, Abundance, and Ease

75

You deserve to be treated with fairness and love by yourself and by others. We are all children of the Universe. No one person is better than another.

76

You know what to do next, even if your mind doesn't. Slow down and allow the voice within to speak. Acting too quickly at this time may not be in your highest good. If you do find yourself in a situation that doesn't support your highest good, acknowledge it, ask to be shown the good in it, bless it, and work at changing direction.

Tips and Tricks for living a life of Joy, Abundance, and Ease

77

Ask Archangel Michael to help you release your fears. He's also great to call on when you feel you're in need of protection or help with releasing anger.

For info on angels, see page iv.

Tips and Tricks for living a life of Joy, Abundance, and Ease

78

Our thoughts are actually prayers to the Universe. If you notice a lower vibrating thought, tell the Universe to cancel it so that it doesn't become part of your reality.

Tips and Tricks for living a life of Joy, Abundance, and Ease

79

View your thoughts as if you are an outside observer to see what is in need of healing.

80

Are your emotions getting the best of you today? Are you being challenged by others? Do you feel as though your foundation is crumbling? Take a couple of deep breaths to center. Then send love to whatever or whoever is challenging you. If you can't find it within you to send love, ask the Universe, Source, Creator, the Angels to do it for you.

Tips and Tricks for living a life of Joy, Abundance, and Ease

81

Sometimes the best way to resolve a conflict is to walk away from it. Let your intuition guide you. Trust that by removing your energy from the situation you're opening doors for greater opportunities.

Tips and Tricks for living a life of Joy, Abundance, and Ease

82

Look for the beauty in all that you do. It brings light and joy to your days... even if it's a fleeting moment.

Tips and Tricks for living a life of Joy, Abundance, and Ease

83

You're always being guided to your True path. Actually, you're already on your True path. It's just that some steps bring you closer to your heart's desire faster, while others may actually be the long way around.

Tips and Tricks for living a life of Joy, Abundance, and Ease

84

Spend a few moments relaxing today and let your imagination run wild. What new dreams can you dream? What miracles can you envision? Have fun and explore the possibilities. You never know what kind of reality you may choose to create as a result.

85

Our lives are similar to the process of creating a painting. Like an artist we begin with an idea, we sketch it out, gather materials, prepare the canvas, and begin to paint. An artist is present in every moment of his work, just as we should be in life. He may not like the process involved with each step, but he loves the results of each one. You can do the same. See yourself and your life as a work of art in progress.

86

You have the opportunity to choose to make adjustments to your life as your vision of it alters.

Tips and Tricks for living a life of Joy, Abundance, and Ease

87

Love who you are during each step in the process of creating your life. Know that who you are is a result of the steps taken so far and are absolutely perfect in that moment.

88

If an ending is at hand, allow it to open the way for something more in alignment with your Truth.

Tips and Tricks for living a life of Joy, Abundance, and Ease

89

What brings you joy? Can you remember? Have you gotten so caught up in the practicalities of life (i.e. work, money, errands, etc.) that you forgot about joy? Take a few minutes to enjoy something today. Admire a flower, watch your fish swim... be completely and totally present and truly enjoy the moment. You deserve to give yourself that gift. You deserve to receive that gift.

Tips and Tricks for living a life of Joy, Abundance, and Ease

90

Keep your eye on the big picture, don't be afraid to ask for help (from the physical world, spiritual world, or both) and allow your dreams to unfold in a way that is perfect for you in this moment.

Tips and Tricks for living a life of Joy, Abundance, and Ease

91

What's your inner voice asking you to do? Does it want you to act in a new way? Is it asking you to take a circuitous route? If you're resisting the request in some way, look at the reasons why. Look at the new ways from a place of love, or at least curiosity. What if the new idea works? What if changing your approach works?

Tips and Tricks for living a life of Joy, Abundance, and Ease

92

Take a few moments to connect with Spirit every day. Take a walk in nature, spend time in meditation, or take a few moments to be in gratitude. It doesn't have to be anything formal or time consuming. Are you sitting still in traffic? Connect. Waiting in the dentist office? Connect. Showering? Connect. You get the picture. Just do it.

Tips and Tricks for living a life of Joy, Abundance, and Ease

93

What happens if you heal? Will you know who you are? Will you know how to interact with others? What will your life look like? Do these questions bring peace and contentment or fear and uncertainty? Many people don't heal because they actually fear the changes that may result. Recognizing this is the first step to removing the fear and clearing the path to healing.

Tips and Tricks for living a life of Joy, Abundance, and Ease

94

Are you living by your definition of responsibility or someone else's? Are you doing what you are "supposed" to do, or what feels right to you? Are you acting in a way that resonates with your soul, or in the way that's expected of you? Are you being true to your Self, or are you behaving the way people believe you "should"?

Tips and Tricks for living a life of Joy, Abundance, and Ease

95

Look for reasons to celebrate and find joy in your life. Stuff happens, but that doesn't mean you are required to remain mired in the muck 24/7/365.

Tips and Tricks for living a life of Joy, Abundance, and Ease

96

Here's a crystal that will help bring the vibration of joy into your life: Crazy lace agate. I call this the stone of laughter. All I have to do is hold it and I'm smiling. In addition, it's said to be a stone that increases energy and stamina. Who doesn't need some of that? Plus, it helps you to remain focused and aids in decision making.

For more info on using crystals, see page iii.

Tips and Tricks for living a life of Joy, Abundance, and Ease

97

Practice being your own best friend instead of your own worst enemy.

Tips and Tricks for living a life of Joy, Abundance, and Ease

98

Are you sending the Universe mixed messages? Denying the help the Universe offers, especially when it's due to fear or the help hasn't come the way you expected, sends a message to the Universe that you don't really want its help or guidance.

Tips and Tricks for living a life of Joy, Abundance, and Ease

99

If your chosen path is filled with suffering, then it's time to try a new direction. Although there will always be bumps in the road, or possibly soul contracts for experiences that aren't easy, your Soul's Purpose is NOT to endlessly suffer.

Tips and Tricks for living a life of Joy, Abundance, and Ease

100

Spirit reminds you to stay connected, to be generous, and selfless in your giving. This includes giving to yourself... doing so in a loving way strengthens your core, your heart, your love, and your light... making it possible for you to continue giving to others without depleting yourself.

Tips and Tricks for living a life of Joy, Abundance, and Ease

101

Persevere and allow the vastness of the Universe and all the miracles it has to offer to unfold.

Tips and Tricks for living a life of Joy, Abundance, and Ease

102

There may be times when even though you're following your destiny you're challenged to the point where you need to rebuild your foundations. How you view those situations is what will create your new reality. Will you be in fear and remain attached to the old, or will you adapt and accept the new? The choice is yours.

Tips and Tricks for living a life of Joy, Abundance, and Ease

103

Call on the Ascended Masters. Trust what you see in your mind's eye and know that the Masters are always available to aide you in your spiritual mission and teach you how best to use your gifts.

Tips and Tricks for living a life of Joy, Abundance, and Ease

104

"I now call forth wonderful experiences that are in the highest good. I don't know what they are or how they will come, but I accept them all. And so it is." Repeat this three times in a row with emotion and watch what unfolds.

Tips and Tricks for living a life of Joy, Abundance, and Ease

105

lue aragonite is a beautiful soft blue stone that's soothing just to look at. This is a great stone for anyone who is dealing with issues of anger. Blue aragonite also helps you to experience joy in all aspects of your life, no matter how hectic or frustrating it may be. If you're an empath, it helps keep you from being overwhelmed by everyone else's emotions. This is also a crystal that helps with lung issues. So grab one of these to keep your chest cold at bay. Finally, this is a stone that helps increase intuition. Meditate with blue aragonite to help open you up to best possible choices.

For more info on using crystals, see page iii.

Tips and Tricks for living a life of Joy, Abundance, and Ease

106

Love and accept what you don't like about yourself as simply a part of who you are. Our shadow sides often offer wisdom we would not otherwise have access to.

Tips and Tricks for living a life of Joy, Abundance, and Ease

107

As you continue your journey toward healing, know that in actuality you are always perfect in every way. We all are.

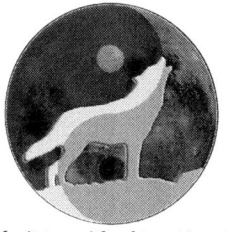

Tips and Tricks for living a life of Joy, Abundance, and Ease

108

Honor the Divine within you and detoxify your Self by releasing people and/or situations that are not in alignment with your authentic self.

Tips and Tricks for living a life of Joy, Abundance, and Ease

109

Giving too much of yourself is often a result of low self worth. Taking without giving comes from a feeling of lack or victimization. There is a natural flow and balance to breathing, each inhale is followed by an exhale. Practice finding your natural flow and balance between giving and receiving.

110

Keep obsessions (including obsessive thoughts and worries) at bay by acquiring True knowledge and asking the Universe to bring clarity to your thoughts and situations.

Tips and Tricks for living a life of Joy, Abundance, and Ease

111

Practice giving your worries to the Universe. Write your concerns on a piece of paper, bless it, rip it up, and burn it. Watch as the smoke carries your worries out to the Universe to be dealt with in the highest way. Throw away the remaining ash, bury it, or send it down the drain.

Tips and Tricks for living a life of Joy, Abundance, and Ease

112

Expressing yourself creatively is a great way to not only feed your soul, but also to heal. Tamping down your creative energies is like suffocating a part of yourself. Open up and let them breathe. Remember, you don't need to be "good" at art, music, painting, etc. You don't even have to show your handiwork to anyone... just find joy in expressing your creative energy.

113

Sometimes a problem is actually an answer to our prayers. Look past the mistakes and misunderstandings and view the situation from a place of love. Forgive yourself for your part of the process, release what's no longer working for you, and don't forget to allow for moments of play. The brief respites will soothe your soul and give you the courage to move on. The process is simple, though it may not be easy.

Tips and Tricks for living a life of Joy, Abundance, and Ease

114

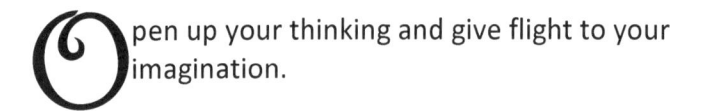

Open up your thinking and give flight to your imagination.

Tips and Tricks for living a life of Joy, Abundance, and Ease

115

Imagine what you and your life would look and feel like if you lived without fear.

Tips and Tricks for living a life of Joy, Abundance, and Ease

116

Let go of fear and welcome the unknown.

Tips and Tricks for living a life of Joy, Abundance, and Ease

117

Learn and experience how to love yourself by continuing to let go of belief patterns that no longer serve you. The more you clear them, the more love you allow into your life. More love allows more experiences that serve your highest good and highest purpose.

Tips and Tricks for living a life of Joy, Abundance, and Ease

118

Start paying attention to how you value yourself. Are you giving yourself the same amount of love, compassion, and respect that you give others? Are you allowing yourself time to relax and connect with spirit? If you answered 'no' to any of these questions, you might want to look into why.

Tips and Tricks for living a life of Joy, Abundance, and Ease

119

Protecting yourself from your own negative thoughts and fears is an essential part of your life.

Tips and Tricks for living a life of Joy, Abundance, and Ease

120

When you get lost in your "stuff", you create a space where you can't see the truth or yourself.

Tips and Tricks for living a life of Joy, Abundance, and Ease

121

What if your perceived imperfections were actually unique gifts that you have to offer the world?

Tips and Tricks for living a life of Joy, Abundance, and Ease

122

Not everyone is able to accept or receive the unique gifts each of us has to offer. Rather than allowing non-acceptance to devalue your gift, understand that people receive when they are willing, able, and ready.

Tips and Tricks for living a life of Joy, Abundance, and Ease

123

Call on Archangel Gabriel for help with conceiving or adopting a child. She is also the angel to call upon for help if you are in the arts, or if you are an actor, writer, or in any fields related to acting, writing, music, or journalism. If you are experiencing a block in any of these areas, Archangel Gabriel will help you move past it.

For info on angels, see page iv.

124

Oracle cards, spirits, angels, psychics, etc. are all wonderful tools to use to obtain answers. Each acts as a channel for your inner knowing or inner voice.

125

Do you know the difference between being alone versus being lonely? Learning how to do things on your own (like go to a movie or dinner) and be comfortable with yourself while doing them will help enrich your life.

126

Taking a break from the world, communication, even friends and family, can have unexpected results. Practice moments of solitude whenever possible... especially in nature... and notice what you discover about yourself.

Tips and Tricks for living a life of Joy, Abundance, and Ease

127

Breathe... Close your eyes, quiet your mind, and take a few deep breaths. Ahhhh...

128

The Source of all Healing is unconditional love.

Tips and Tricks for living a life of Joy, Abundance, and Ease

129

Call on Archangel Uriel when you need clarity. He's there to bring in wisdom and new perspectives. He's always willing to shed light on your situation.

For info on angels, see page iv.

Tips and Tricks for living a life of Joy, Abundance, and Ease

130

Although all things are possible, some are more probable than others. What can you do to increase the probabilities of the experiences you'd like to have?

Tips and Tricks for living a life of Joy, Abundance, and Ease

131

Take a short break from your problems by letting your inner child out to create something beautiful. You don't think you're creative? Putting flowers in a vase is creating, smiling at someone is creating, daydreaming is creating. Let the heart of your inner child choose the creation and find the joy in it.

132

Impossible and Improbable. Do you know the difference? How often do you use the word impossible, when you really mean improbable?

Tips and Tricks for living a life of Joy, Abundance, and Ease

133

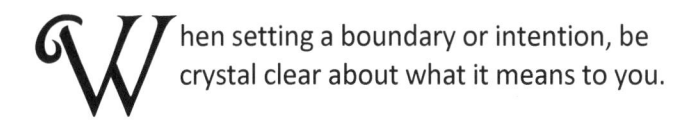

When setting a boundary or intention, be crystal clear about what it means to you.

Tips and Tricks for living a life of Joy, Abundance, and Ease

134

There are times when you may feel the need to visit your old self and engage in behaviors that no longer serve. When you do, remember it's just a visit... it may be "fun" for a little while, but it won't hold the same appeal it once did. These reminders help you to remember where you are now... After your visit, let it go, forgive yourself... and continue moving forward.

Tips and Tricks for living a life of Joy, Abundance, and Ease

135

What's triggering you today? A trigger is a wake-up call to look at yourself. There is something within you that needs healing. When you allow other people's "stuff" to trigger you, you are blaming them for your reactions and giving away your power.

136

If you are unwilling to ask for or accept help from others, how can you ask for or accept help from the Universe?

Tips and Tricks for living a life of Joy, Abundance, and Ease

137

Pay attention to your ideas today. Messages are often received in the form of thoughts and ideas. How do they make you feel? A thought or idea that's in alignment with your soul will never ask you to be untrue to yourself.

138

Stop "trying" and just "do" it. Changing the way you phrase an action can make a huge difference in how you view your progress. "I'm trying to_____" can be rephrased as "I'm working on_____". You've now taken your action from failure to success.

Tips and Tricks for living a life of Joy, Abundance, and Ease

139

Love in all its forms is the key to manifesting the life you desire. Allow it to shed light and bring forth hidden details. Look for messages from Spirit to guide you on your way.

Tips and Tricks for living a life of Joy, Abundance, and Ease

140

The time to be true to yourself is now. Being true to yourself can be uncomfortable at first, both for you and others. Ask yourself why you're uncomfortable. Then decide what, if anything, you're going to do about it.

Tips and Tricks for living a life of Joy, Abundance, and Ease

141

Have you been listening to your guides and angels? Watch for synchronicities and odd occurrences. Synchronicities arise to help us know which direction to take.

Tips and Tricks for living a life of Joy, Abundance, and Ease

142

If something doesn't feel right, then it's probably not right for you. Honor and love yourself just as you are, and you will attract people and situations that do fit and do feel right.

Tips and Tricks for living a life of Joy, Abundance, and Ease

143

It's not natural to never have a negative thought. When you do, telling the Universe to cancel it will reduce and even negate the power behind it.

144

Embracing the shadow side helps one to become whole. Ask the Universe to show you how to love, respect, and have compassion for your entire self.

Tips and Tricks for living a life of Joy, Abundance, and Ease

145

If you can't give yourself the gift of love, it makes it difficult to receive it from others.

Tips and Tricks for living a life of Joy, Abundance, and Ease

146

The Universe has heard your call for help... watch for the answers in the form of new beginnings. It's time to step into the next chapter of your life.

Tips and Tricks for living a life of Joy, Abundance, and Ease

147

What do you do to feed and nurture your soul? If you can't answer this question with little to no hesitation, then chances are your soul is in need of some TLC. Paint, write, sing, dance, take a walk outside... but be present while doing it. Pay attention to sights, sounds, feelings. Soak it in and feel your soul expand.

148

Everyone and everything is sacred. This has nothing to do with opinions or personal taste. The more you are able to see the sacredness in the world around you (including yourself), the more enjoyable and easy your life becomes. Challenges will still arise, but the drama attached to them will be far less.

Tips and Tricks for living a life of Joy, Abundance, and Ease

149

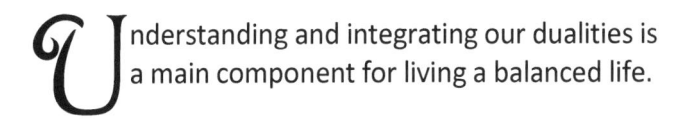

Understanding and integrating our dualities is a main component for living a balanced life.

Tips and Tricks for living a life of Joy, Abundance, and Ease

150

Honor the beautiful being that you are.

Tips and Tricks for living a life of Joy, Abundance, and Ease

Robin Linke is a modern-day healer for our changing times who provides her clients with restoration, calm, and peace – helping to pave the way for magic and miracles!

Robin is a Master Energy Therapist, ThetaHealing® Practitioner, Reiki Master Teacher, Angelic Integrated Energy Therapy® Master-Instructor, Intuitive Crystal Healer, Author and Intuitive. She has also created the Angel and Gemstone Guidance Card Deck and designs energy-infused healing jewelry.

To purchase products and services,
please visit Robin's website at
www.RobinLinke.com

Made in the USA
Charleston, SC
10 February 2012